BRIDGES TO RELIGIONS

THE WARWICK RE PROJECT

The Seventh Day is Shabbat

Written by Margaret Barratt

Series editors: Judith Everington and Robert Jackson

Acknowledgements
Thanks are due to Jacob's family and to the Jewish Community in Birmingham; the Head Teacher, staff and pupils of King David School, Birmingham; and Peter Woodward.

Thanks are due to the following for the use of original photographs: Noel Barratt, front and back cover, pp.1, 4–12, 15–17; Peter Roberts, p.14, 19–23; Peter Woodward, pp.13, 18.

First published 1994

98 97 96 95 94
10 9 8 7 6 5 4 3 2 1

British Cataloguing in Publication Data
A catalogue record for this book is available from the British Library

ISBN 0 435 30407 0 (One each of 5 titles)
ISBN 0 435 30405 4 (5 x The Seventh Day is Shabbat, Paperback)
ISBN 0 431 07733 9 (The Seventh Day is Shabbat, Hardback)

Heinemann Educational Publishers,
A Division of Heinemann Publishers (Oxford) Ltd,
Halley Court, Jordan Hill, Oxford OX2 8EJ

OXFORD LONDON EDINBURGH
MADRID ATHENS BOLOGNA PARIS
MELBOURNE SYDNEY AUCKLAND SINGAPORE
TOKYO IBADAN NAIROBI HARARE
GABORONE PORTSMOUTH NH (USA)

Designed and typeset by Green Door Design Ltd
Printed in Hong Kong

Contents

Special Words

Capel (Pronounced capple)
A special skull cap worn by men and boys

Hallah (Pronounced chal-ah – the ch as in loch)
Special bread

Havdalah (Pronounced have-dah-lah)
A goodbye ceremony

Kiddush (Pronounced kid-oosh)
The blessing over the wine

Shabbat (Pronounced Sha-bat)
The seventh day, a special holiday

Shul (Pronounced shool)
A place to worship God

Torah (Pronounced Tor-rah)
A special scroll book

Jacob is Jewish.
He wears a special hat, called a capel.
He wears it on his favourite day.
The day is called Shabbat.

Jacob says, “Shabbat is the day God rested after making the world.” It begins each Friday evening and lasts until Saturday night. It is a holiday for Jewish people.

At Jacob's school, the children act out the Shabbat celebration. Jacob is proud to be chosen to join in. Jacob gets two candles to show that Shabbat is a bright happy time.

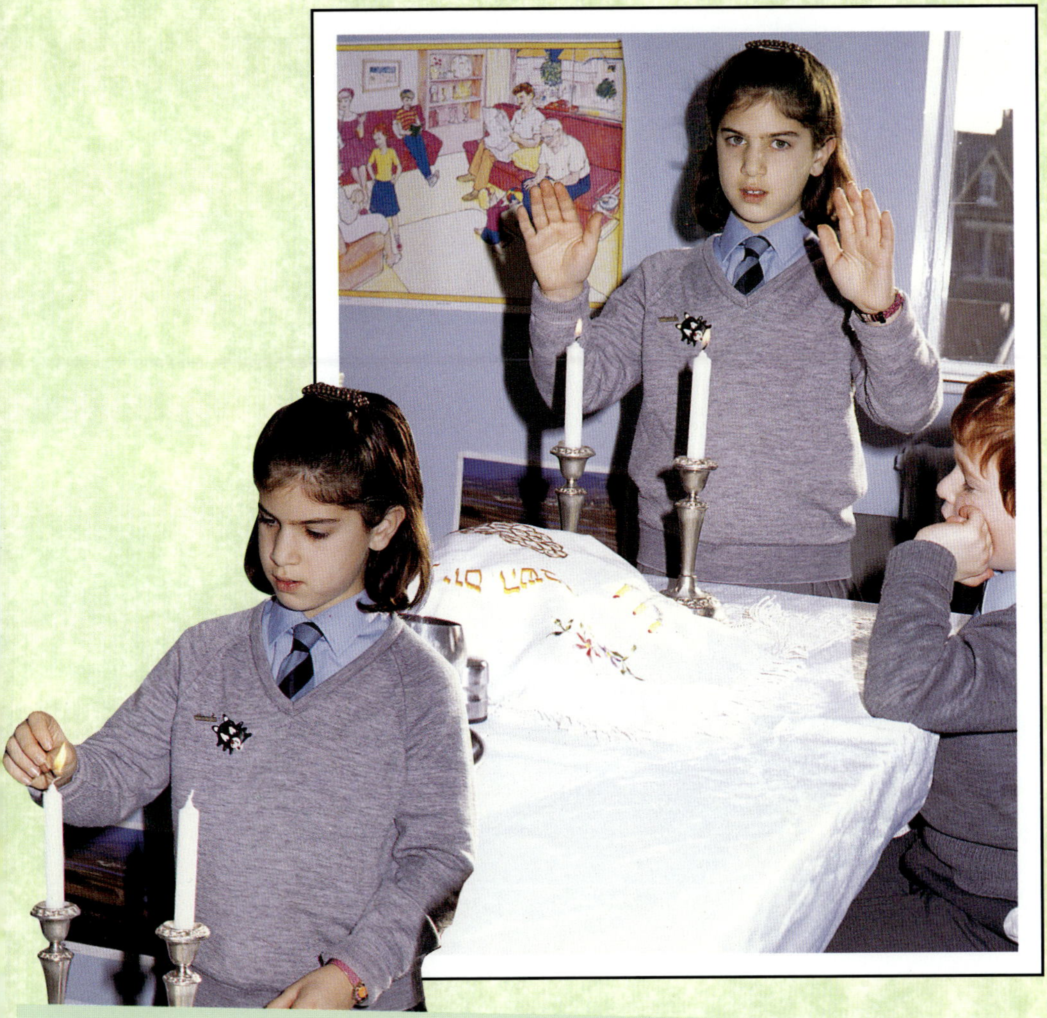

Jacob's sister, Sarah, acts as Mother.
She lights the Shabbat candles.
She moves her hands in circles.
She says a prayer to welcome
the special day.

Jacob's friend, Baruch, acts as Father.
He pours the 'wine'.
It is really fruit juice.
Baruch reads out the blessing called kiddush and everyone drinks.

The children wash their hands.
They use a special cup.
Then they are ready to
share the blessing of the bread.
The special bread is called hallah.

Baruch has uncovered the two loaves.
Long ago God promised the Jews
a new land.
He gave them food on their journey.
He gave them extra for Shabbat.

Baruch says a blessing for
the hallah and then he cuts it.
Jacob reminds Baruch to
sprinkle salt on it like Dad does.
They give hallah to everyone.

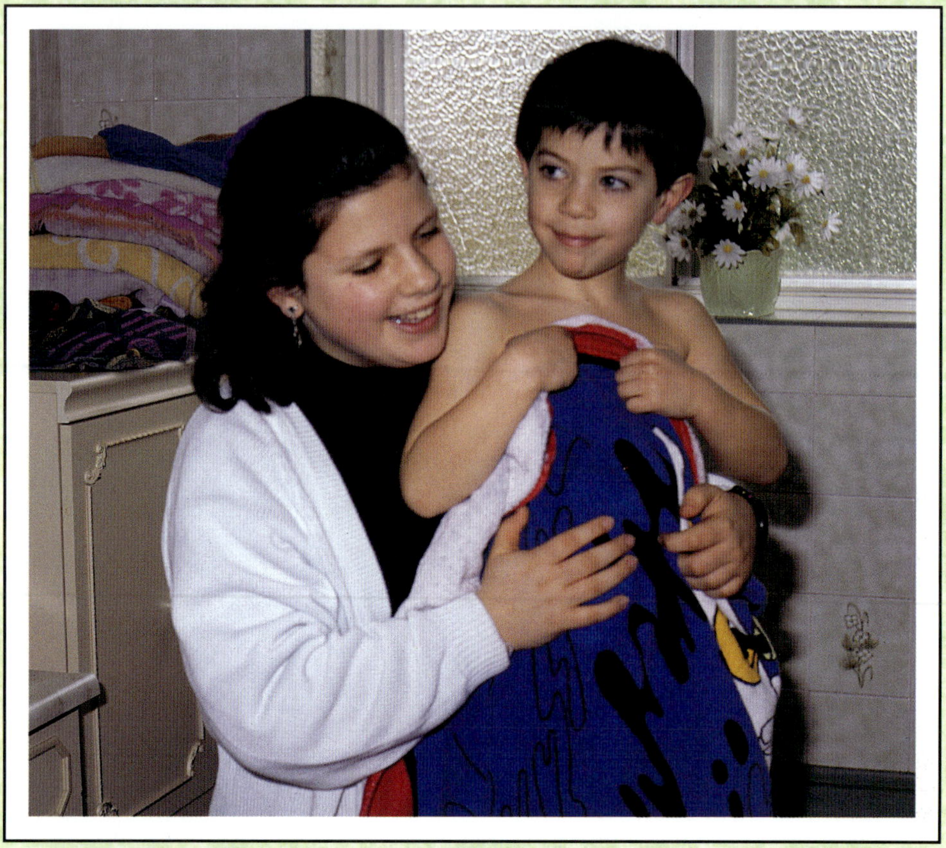

After school it is time for the real Shabbat.
Jacob's big sister, Emily, helps him with his bath.
He puts on clean clothes.

Before Shabbat Mum is always
busy in the kitchen.
She uses her best things.
It's like having a special
visitor to a party.

Dad comes home and Mum lights the Shabbat candles.
Then Dad blesses all the children.
Dad speaks some nice words about Mum.
The family begin their lovely meal.

They talk and sing.
Jacob joins in.
When he gets tired he climbs
on to Dad's lap.

On Saturday it is still Shabbat. Jacob walks through the park to shul. The flowers remind him of the story of how God made the whole world in only six days.

Shul is the building where
Jacob's family worships God.
They don't go in the car.
Dad knows it is wrong for a
Jew to drive a car on Shabbat.

At shul Jacob goes to
the children's service.
The children have their own ark where
they keep their own Torah.
It has God's law written in it.

Later the children join
the grown-ups.
Jacob sits downstairs with his
dad and his big brother.
His sisters sit upstairs with Mum.

When they get home they do not do any work.

Mum reads the newspaper.

When Dad's had a rest he plays games with the children.

When it's time for Shabbat to end
Jacob holds up the havdalah candle.
Havdalah is a blessing.
It shows it's the end of
Shabbat for this week.

Everyone in the family smells the spice box.
Jacob thinks it has a strong smell.
Mum says it helps you keep the peaceful Shabbat feeling all week.

Dad pours out some wine until
it overflows.
He puts out the candle flame.
They say “Goodbye” to Shabbat until
the seventh day comes again.

Index